GUIDE WITH
RECONSTRUCTIONS

ANCIENT ATHENS

CAPE SOUNION, AEGINA,
AND OLYMPIA

past and
present

Delphi

Ithaka

MARATHON

Cephallenia

Zacynthus

Mycenae

OLYMPIA

ATHENS

CORINTH

AEGINA

EPIDAURUS

CAPE SOUNION

Sparta

Cythera

Crete

INDEX

ATHENS

ITS LIFE AND HISTORY 3

The Ancient City 10
A walk on the Acropolis 11
The Propylaia 15
The Parthenon 21
The Erechtheion 28
The Theater of Dionysos 32
Walking along the Peripatos 36
The Odeion of Herodes Atticus 39
The Pnyx, the Areopagus,
the Hill of the Nymphs and the Hill
of the Muses 40
The Kerameikos district 44
The Agora 47
The Olympieion 56
A visit to the Museums 59

CAPE SOUNION 63

AEGINA 67

OLYMPIA

HISTORY OF THE SANCTUARY 73

The Altis 75
The Nymphaeum of Herodes Atticus 84
The Heraion 86
The Philippeion 88
The Temple of Zeus 90

ATHENS

The city of Athens stands in the center of a vast plain surrounded by the heights of Mount Hymettos, Mount Pentelikon, Mount Parnes and Mount Aigaleos and opening out onto the Saronic Gulf to the south. The first settlement was located on the Acropolis and in the level area around the rock, and on the hills a short distance away from it to the southwest: the Hill of the Muses (Mouseion), the Pnyx, the Hill of the Nymphs and the Areopagus. The eastern part of the city was crossed by the River Ilissos, and the northern part by the River Eridanos. The first traces date back to the Neolithic Age (6500–4500 B.C.).

In Mycenean times (1600–1100 B.C.) Athens was the capital of a kingdom, with a palace within the walls that enclosed the citadel. Traces of the Mycenean fortification known as the Pelargikon are partially visible on the slopes of the Acropolis.

According to literary tradition, the expansion of Athens was due to Theseus, the mythical civilizing hero who brought about the so-called synecism (union) of Attica during his reign in the middle of the XIIIth century B.C. This encouraged the unification of Attica by grouping the inhabitants of the region, who were divided into four tribes, under the city of Athens. This process probably took place in the Archaic age, in the eighth century B.C.

Government was by a king until the time of Kodros, who committed suicide when the oracle pronounced that the city would be saved from invasion by the Dori-

Limestone pediment from the Acropolis with a triple-bodied monster; mid 6th century B.C.

The "Flautist", Cycladic marble figurine (Athens, National Museum)

ans only if the king was dead. The Athenians, convinced they would never find a successor worthy of him, decided to give up the monarchy.

From then onwards the city was in the hands of nobles, the Eupatridai, from whose ranks magistrates termed *archontes* were elected. Their office initially lasted for life, and then 10 years. Finally it was reduced to an annual office from the 680s onwards. Of the history of Athens during this period, we know of Kylon's unsuccessful coup d'état (630 B.C.) and the figure of the lawmaker Drako, who in 620 B.C. passed legislation concerning criminal law which included a distinction between murder and manslaughter.

The most eminent figure was nonetheless that of Solon, *arihon* in 594 B.C.; some of

his poetry survives. He passed a series of reforms touching upon various areas: the abolition of agrarian debt and the liberation of those enslaved due to debts deriving from the system of land ownership; the institution of the court of the Heliaea (open to all those Athenian citizens aged over thirty) and reform of the system of weights and measures.

Solon is also credited with the creation of the Council of the Four Hundred (the *Boule*), and the division by census of the Athenian population. Previously there had been three classes, the *eupatridai* (aristocrats), the *geomoroi* (farmers) and the *demiourgoi* (those who lived from their own work). Solon introduced

Portrait of Solon, Roman copy (Florence, Uffizi Gallery)

a fourth class (*medimnoi*), with membership established on the basis of each man's income from land, fixed in measures of cereals.

In 561 B.C. the tyrant Peisistratos came to power, and was succeeded by his sons Hippias and Hipparchos. The period of rule by this family was an important period in Athenian history, and not only from the point of view of the city's development. During this time Athens started to mint its own coinage, which, alongside that of Aegina and Corinth, is the most ancient coinage of the whole of Greece. In 508 Kleisthenes established a democratic regime in the city.

In the early fifth century Athens became involved in the struggle against the Persians. Cyrus, king of the Persians, had conquered the Greek colonies on the coast of Asia Minor, and Miletus had headed a revolt, for which it had obtained the help of the Greeks. After the destruction of Miletus in 494 B.C., Cyrus's successor, Darius, sent a punitive expedition to Greece, where he was defeated at the Battle of Marathon in 490 B.C. Ten years later, Xerxes sent a new expedition that, arriving via the Hellespont and Thessaly, defeated the Spartan army at Thermopylae and reached as far as Attica, taking control of the Acropolis in Athens. The Athenian fleet then won a naval battle against the Persians at Salamis in 480 B.C., and in the following year the Persian army was also defeated at Plataea by the joint forces of Athenians and Spartans. In 461 B.C.

Portrait of Perikles, Roman copy (Rome, Vatican Museum)

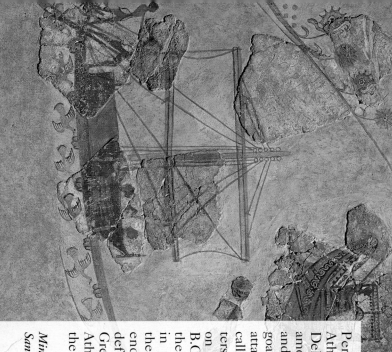

Perikles came to power in Athens. The city headed the Delian-Attic League, an alliance among the cities of the Aegean and Asia Minor which had as its goal the common defence against attacks from Persia, and was so called because its first headquarters was the Sanctuary of Apollo on Delos. Between 422 and 431 B.C. Athens and Sparta found themselves fighting each other in the long conflict known as the Peloponnesian War, which ended in 404 B.C. with the defeat of Athens. A new phase in Greek history then began, with Athens losing her hegemony in the Greek world, to the extent

Minoan fresco of a naval fleet from Santorini, detail

that soon after the defeat of the Athenians in the Battle of Chaironeia by the Macedonians, a Macedonian garrison was installed in Athens and the city also lost its fleet (War of Lamia, 322 B.C.). Soon after, Rome also began to intervene in Greece. In 197 B.C., Titus Quinctius Flamininus proclaimed all Greek cities free from the Macedonian yoke, but this freedom was relative, given Rome's interference in Greek affairs. When the Macedonians attempted to regain control of part of Greece, the Romans defeated them at Pydna (168 B.C.), and Macedon became a Roman province. Soon after, in 146 B.C., the Romans sacked Corinth, once again proclaiming themselves saviors of Greece, but in reality this freedom was only nominal. The Greek cities attempted to rebel alongside Mithridates King of Pontus, and the consequence of this rebellion was the extremely harsh repression applied by the

Roman general Sulla, who conquered Athens in 86 B.C. after destroying Delos. From then on Greece was definitively in the hands of Rome.

In the first two centuries of the Empire, Athens was still able to enjoy a relative degree of autonomy and to flourish, thanks to the philhellenism of certain emperors such as Hadrian. But in A.D. 267 it was invaded by the barbarian people known as the Heruli, with devastating consequences.

The city was rebuilt and became the seat of schools of philosophy in the fifth century A.D. When these closed as a result of Justinian's edict of A.D. 527, the city was the capital of an *eparchia* (administrative unit) of the Byzantine empire.

It was then occupied by the Franks until the mid-15th century, and by the Turks until 1821, becoming capital of the Greek state in 1833.

After the liberation from the Turks, the archaeological excavations started with the elimination of the medieval structures that had swallowed up the monuments of the ancient city, especially on the Acropolis, which was used as a stronghold. A little earlier, still under Turkish rule, the British consul Lord Elgin had removed the marble sculptures that decorated the Parthenon; they are now exhibited at the British Museum in London. In addition to information provided by literary sources, recent projects for the construction of new underground lines and infrastructure related to the staging of the 2004 Olympic Games have made it possible to broaden our knowledge of the city's layout and monuments.

Detail of the entablature of the west facade of the Parthenon

THE ANCIENT CITY

Athens is surrounded by walls that date back to the Mycenean period. Traces of these fortifications are still visible on the southwestern side of the Acropolis. A lost ring of walls mentioned by the historian Thucydides must have been built in the sixth century, perhaps under Solon or more probably during the tyranny of Peisistratos.

After the Persian invasion of 480/479 B.C., the so-called Wall of Themistokles was built. This encircles a large part of the city, from the course of the Eridanos to the hills of the Pnyx, Nymphs,

Relief with ball game (Athens, National Museum)

and Muses. There were several gates in this enceinte, which took their names from the role they played (Sacred Gate, Hippades Gate) or from the direction of the roads leading away from them out of the city (Acharnian Gate, Peiraic Gate). The Wall of Themistokles, which was destroyed by the Spartans in 404 B.C. at the end of the Peloponnesian War, was rebuilt by Konon in 394 B.C.

A new enceinte was raised in Athens during the reign of Valerian (A.D. 252–260) and rebuilt after the invasion of the Heruli in A.D. 267.

A walk on the Acropolis

The Acropolis is the heart of the city of Athens. It is a steep limestone crag (156 meters/512 feet above sea level) where,

Aerial view of the Acropolis

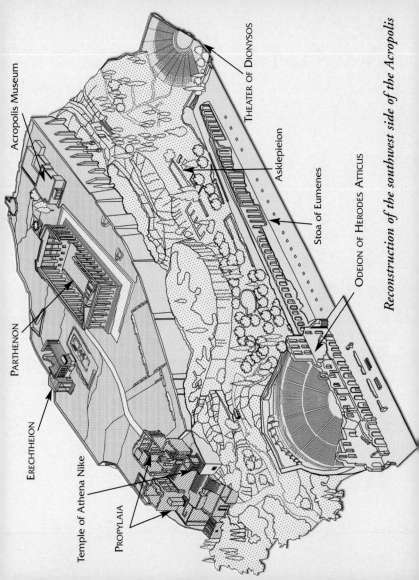

Acropolis Museum

PARTHENON

ERECHTHEION

Temple of Athena Nike

PROPYLAIA

THEATER OF DIONYSOS

Asklepieion

ODEION OF HERODES ATTICUS

Stoa of Eumenes

Reconstruction of the southwest side of the Acropolis

during the Pisistratid era, in the second half of the sixth century B.C., the first religious buildings were raised on the fortified site of the Mycenean palace and the shrines of the Geometric period (eighth century B.C.). When Peisistratos instituted the celebrations in honor of the goddess Athena, known as the Greater Panathenaea, he consecrated an altar to Athena Nike (Victory). A ramp was built, across which the procession could ascend the Acropolis, site of the first temples: the Hekatompedon (Temple of a Hundred Feet) in 570-566 B.C., in the area where the Parthenon was later to stand, and the Temple of Athena, in the 520s.

The original Propylon (ornamental gateway of entry to a sacred or public area) and a small temple built in the local limestone (*poros*) next to the altar of Athena Nike both date to the years of the Persian Wars (490–480 B.C.). During this period, the Hekatompedon was dismantled, and work on the Parthenon began, but it was not completed, due to the Persian invasion of 480 B.C. After this, the architectural pieces, statues and reliefs of the sacred buildings, which had been contaminated by enemy hands according to the Athenians, were buried in a large ditch. This is known as the "Persian landfill," and is very important for our knowledge of the history of Greek art. Indeed, it represents a fixed point of reference for the dating of the works it contains, which must have been produced prior to the destruction of the Acropolis by Xerxes's army. The Acropolis was reconsecrated and rebuilt from 448 B.C. onwards, after the signing of the treaty of peace between Athens and the Persians (the "Peace of Kallias," which was actually negotiated by Perikles).

THE PROPYLAIA

During the reconstruction of the Periclean period, the monumental entrance was redesigned by the architect Mnesikles and given the name of Propylaia. This is a monument in Pentelic marble dedicated to the goddess Athena, consisting of a central body with six Doric columns on the façade and two colonnaded wings, one of which was known as the "picture gallery" as it contained several pictures (*pinakes*).

A further transformation of the entrance to the Acropolis was undertaken in the first century A.D., during the reign of the emperor Claudius, when the ramp up which the Panathenaic Procession ascended the Acropolis was substituted with a broad stairway.

Entering the façade, visitors went through

The Acropolis from north-west side

the Propylaia, proceeding on a ramp flanked by columns, with five portals and ceilings of marble coffering, to the sides of which were monuments donated to the sanctuary by important figures (*donaria*). These monuments included the statue of Aphrodite Sosandra (savior of men), a 460 B.C. work by the sculptor Kalamis; the Propylaia Hermes by Alkamenes; and the relief depicting the Three Graces by the sculptor Sokrates. Having passed through the Propylaia, one reached the level area of the Acropolis, where there were several other *donaria* and votive statues, including

The Propylaia, detail of the colonnade

The Propylaia in the 5ᵗʰ century B.C., reconstruction

the Athena Lemnia (offered by the inhabitants of the island of Lemnos in the north Aegean) and the Athena Promachos ("champion in battle") by the famous sculptor Pheidias.

In the southwest corner of the Acropolis stands the **Temple of Athena Nike** (built on the site of the temple to the same divinity erected by Peisistratos), a building with four Ionic columns across the front and the same number behind, in which was kept the wooden statue of the cult, representing the goddess with a pomegranate in her right hand and a helmet in her left one. The temple was also known as the Temple of Nike Apteros (unwinged Victory) because the statue's wings of gold had been stolen.

Temple of Athena Nike from the east

Reconstruction of the Propylaia in the 1ˢᵗ century A.D.

The building, which is the work of the architect Kallikrates, was built between the mid-fifth century and 421 B.C. We know that the pediment was decorated with bronze *acroteria* (statues placed on top of the pediment) depicting Bellerophon (the mythical hero who killed the Chimaera) and flying Victories, and that the sculptures represented scenes of *gigantomachia* (battle against Giants) and *amazonomachia* (battle against Amazons). On the continuous Ionic frieze were sculpted scenes of battle and a series of standing deities, in the center of which are Zeus and Poseidon, together with Athena. The temple has been the object of several reconstructions over the last two centuries, the last of which was in recent times. In front of the temple is the altar upon which sacrifices in honor of the goddess were celebrated. One of these ceremonies (the killing of a heifer) is depicted on the relief of the balustrade marking the boundary of the precinct.

"Mourning Athena", ca. 470-450 B.C.
(Athens, Acropolis Museum)

THE PARTHENON

In the south area of the Acropolis stands the Parthenon, built by the architects Kallikrates and Iktinos between the mid-fifth century and A.D. 432, using marble from the quarries of the nearby Mount Pentelikon. The Parthenon, which is generally regarded as the Temple of Athena Parthenos, is actually a huge *donarium* (monumental offering) built to house the colossal chryselephantine statue of the goddess (i.e. in gold and ivory) and the temple treasury. Both Doric and Ionic orders coexist on the building on the outside and inside respectively.

The temple rests on a base of three steps, with a *peristasis* (external colonnade) of 8 columns across the short sides and 17 down the long ones surrounding the 30

Parthenon, detail of the northwest corner

meter (100-foot) long cell. Here we may appreciate such artifices as the very slight curvature of the base, the swelling of the trunks of the columns, and the larger dimensions of the corner columns, identified as "optical corrections" designed to harmonize the view of the building from the perspective of the human eye. The columns bore the architrave and the Doric frieze, composed of *triglyphs* (panels decorated with three grooves) alternating with *metopes* (rectangular panels) depicting the Battle against the Amazons on the west side, the Sack of Troy on the

Deities, from the east frieze of the Parthenon

Fight between a Greek and an Amazon. Roman marble copy from the shield of Pheidias's Athena Parthenos

Parthenon and Erechtheion, reconstruction

north side, the Battle against the Centaurs on the south side, and the Battle against the Giants on the eastern facade. The pediments are the work of Pheidias. One of these depicts the contest between Athena and Poseidon for the dominion of Attica, won by Athena with the gift of an olive tree. On the other is the birth of Athena from the head of Zeus as the gods of Olympus watch on.

The wall of the cell, separated from the outer colonnade by a corridor, is decorated with a continuous frieze depicting the solemn procession, which, on the occasion of the Greater Panathenaea, the celebrations in honor of Athena which took place every four years, concluded with the offering to the goddess of a *peplos* (robe) woven by girls of the aristocratic families of Athens. Instead of the

opisthodomos (the back room of the temple), there was a space with four columns in the middle, the real *parthenon*, where the temple treasure was guarded. The *naos* (cell) was divided into three aisles by rows of columns. In the central aisle, at the back, stood the chryselephantine statue of Athena (about 12 meters/39 feet high), the work of Pheidias, with which we are familiar from Roman-period copies.

This represented Athena in arms, with a Nike (Victory) in her right hand. The helmet of the goddess was decorated with sphinxes, and the shield depicted scenes of battles against Amazons and Centaurs. The soles of the goddess's sandals were also decorated with scenes of battle against the Centaurs. The myth of Pandora was depicted on the base of the

Interior of the Parthenon with the statue of Athena Parthenos of Pheidias, reconstruction

statue. Forty-four talents (about 1140 kilograms/2,508 pounds) of gold were used in its construction, and the cost to the city was 700 talents, the price of a fleet of 230 ships. Alongside the temple, on the north side of the Acropolis, there are slight traces of **monumental offerings** that were famous in antiquity: the foundation of the base of a statue of Gaia (goddess of the earth) and an *exedra* (semicircular recess) originally

Riders from north frieze of Parthenon

containing the statue of Konon, who rebuilt Athens's outer wall in the fourth century B.C.Nearby is the round **Temple of Rome and Augustus**, referred to as a *monopteros*, which was probably consecrated in 19 B.C.

The east sector of the Acropolis was occupied by the **Temple of Zeus Polieus** (guardian of the city) and by the Pandionion (a place of worship of the Attic hero Pandion), but no substantial traces of these monuments remain. Of the Pandionion, a perimeter fence, divided into two parts, entered through a *propylon*, has been identi-

North frieze, detail of a sacrificial procession

The Hydriophoroi (vase-bearers)

fied. Of the temple of Zeus Polieus, there remain incisions in the rock indicating the existence of the outer fence and the altar where the sacrifice in honor of the god took place. The sacrifice, known as the *bouphonia*, involved the killing of an ox with a two-bladed axe followed by a trial, during which the axe was sentenced guilty of the killing and thrown into the sea.

THE ERECHTHEION

In the northern part of the Acropolis stood the Erechtheion. The temple takes its name from Poseidon Erechtheus, the mythical king of Attica, but it is actually the Temple of Athena Polias (guardian of the city) and it is also the place of worship of other ancient deities

Erechtheion, detail of the colonnade

of Athens. The wooden statue of worship of Athena stood in one part of the cell; the other part was divided into three areas and contained the altars of Poseidon and Erichthonios (the half-man, half-serpent son of Hephaistos and Mother Earth), who was protected by Athena), Hephaistos, and the Attic hero Boutes. In the small precinct devoted to the nymph Pandrosos, situated in another part of the temple, grew the olive tree sacred to Athena. A stairway led from the precinct of Pandrosos to the tomb of Kekrops, the mythical king of Athens. The temple, built in the last 20 years of the fifth century B.C. over the remains of two older temples, has an unusual design compared to other Greek temples because it was

Caryatid porch of Erechtheion

designed to house several cults; its position in a very craggy part of the Acropolis is also unusual. The central body consists of the cell, which is divided into two sectors and preceded by an Ionic colonnade consisting of six columns. Behind the cell is the precinct of Pandrosos. On the north side there is a portico containing an altar. Here, according to tradition, Poseidon is supposed to have pointed his trident and made a fountain of pure water spring up, on the occasion of the contest with Athena for the possession of Attica. On the east side is another portico, known as the Porch of the Caryatids, in which six statues of girls support the architrave in place of columns. Due to pollution, the statues have been replaced with

Detail of the bronze statue of Poseidon from Cape Artemision

Erechtheion: reconstruction of the southeast side

plaster casts; the originals are kept in the Acropolis Museum, with the exception of one, which is in the British Museum in London.

THE THEATER OF DIONYSOS

On the southern slopes of the Acropolis, proceeding from east to west, we encounter the remains of the **Odeion of Perikles**, a rectangular building originally covered by a pitched roof, designed for the execution of musical contests.

Further ahead is the **Sanctuary of Dionysos**, the initial plan of which is thought to date back to the age of Peisistratos. The sanctuary consists of a *temenos* (sacred precinct) that contains the god's Doric tem-

Theater of Dyonisos, stage: detail with figure of Silenos

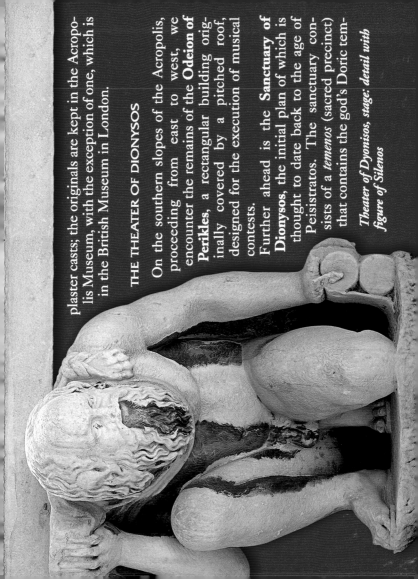

ple, distyle *in antis* (i.e., with two columns on the front and the walls of the cell brought up to their level on either side), in front of which is the altar.

The fourth century B.C. saw the construction alongside the temple of a *stoa* (portico) and another Doric temple, this one *tetrastyle* (with four columns on the front), which contained the sacred gold-and-ivory statue of the god, sculpted by Alkamenes.

To the north of the precinct was the large **Theater of Dionysos**, where theatrical performances took place (tragedies and comedies were sung and danced) during the celebrations in honor of the god.

The theater had a capacity for an audience of about 17,000. It was rebuilt in the fourth century by the orator Lykourgos, and consisted of a big semi-circular *cavea* (a semi-circular space where the spectators sat, originally on wooden benches and then on limestone steps) carved out of the rock; a circular *orchestra* (the area for the circular dancers); and a rectangular stage building. The first row of seats was reserved for those spectators who, by decree of the assembly, enjoyed the right of *proedria*

The musical contest between Apollo and Marsyas

(i.e., the right to sit in the front row during the contests of tragedies; they had marble seats, some of which can still be seen *in situ.*

Statues of the great tragic poets of the fifth century—Aeschylus, Sophocles and Euripides—were erected in the theater by Lykourgos. Some alterations, such as the marble paving in the orchestra, date to the time of the Roman emperor Nero, who famously sang in this theater in A.D. 61.

The *proscaenium* (the stage) is decorated with reliefs depicting the myth of Dionysos and his cult; images include the birth of the god, the characters making up his attendance, and gods and heroes paying homage to him.

Theater mask (Athens, National Museum)

Theater of Dionysos: reconstruction

Theater of Dionysos, Hadrianic frieze of the scene-building with events from the life of the god

Walking along the Peripatos

On the rocky wall of the Acropolis, behind the theater and the sanctuary of Dionysos, runs an ancient road known as the *peripatos*, which flanks the southern and eastern sides of the Acropolis. Along it are the remains of ancient places of worship: the sanctuaries of Gaia Kourotrophos (Earth, rearer of children), Demeter Chloe (protectress of the crops), Aphrodite Pandemos (of all the people), and Isis, as well as the altars of Aphrodite, Hermes, and the Nymphs. In this area are visible a column with a triangular capital and a monument consisting of a facade with three columns located at the entrance to a cave. These are "choregic" monuments, meaning the bases upon which were placed the tripods given as a prize to the organizers (*choregoi*) of the musical contests. Another of these monuments, the

Tripod of Lysikrates, in the form of a circular temple, may be seen not far from the archaeological area, along the road which is still called the Street of the Tripods, on the eastern slopes of the Acropolis in the neighborhood of Plaka.

Proceeding west, we walk along the **Stoa of Eumenes**, a portico a little under 170 meters (558 feet) commissioned by Eumenes II King of Pergamon, who reigned in the first half of the second century B.C.

The portico was on two stories, its facade consisting of a colonnade of 64 Doric columns, and it was divided into two aisles by a colonnade of 31 columns, Ionic on the ground floor and Pergamene on the upper one.

Monument of the choregos Lysikrates, 335 B.C.

Stoa of Eumenes

According to Vitruvius (the Roman author of a history of architecture written in the late Republican period), the building served as a shelter for the theater audience in case of bad weather. Further on, after the Stoa of Eumenes, is the **Odeion of Herodes Atticus.**

THE ODEION OF HERODES ATTICUS

A little after the middle of the second century A.D., this building was commissioned by the very wealthy Athenian citizen Herodes Atticus as a gift to the city. With a capacity for an audience of five thousand, the completely restored theater is still used for concerts and theater productions. It had a semicircular *cavea* in marble from Mount Hymettos, divided into two sectors by a *diazoma* (walkway). The *orchestra* features paving in coloured marble. The stage building was almost 30 meters (98 feet)

Odeion of Herodes Atticus, view of the cavea

high, and its facade, which is organized on three levels, was decorated with columns and niches for statues. It was covered by a roof with beams of Lebanese cedar.

Nearby stood the **Asklepieion**, the Temple of Asklepios, god of medicine. The Sanctuary of Asklepios was built in 418 B.C. near a spring, as is usually the case with deities associated with health. The sacred area of the sanctuary contains the Doric Temple of Asklepios and his co-divine companion, Hygieia, which has four columns across the facade, an altar, and a two-story portico, the Enkoimeterion, where the faithful slept and received from the god the dreams that would heal them. In the northwest area of the portico was a well surrounded by columns, around which the rituals of the *heroa* celebrations in honor of the heroes probably

took place. To the east of the spring is another building, with banqueting halls and a portico of Ionic columns, recognized as the *katagogion* (resting place), a characteristic feature of the sanctuaries of Asklepios. On the western slopes of the Acropolis is a cave close to which must have been the Sanctuary of Aglauros, daughter of Erechtheus, King of Athens; we know from sources that the Prytaneion (where the fire of Hestia was kept) and other important public monuments of the Archaic period were near the Sanctuary of Aglauros.

The Pnyx, the Areopagus, the Hill of the Nymphs, and the Hill of the Muses

Next to the rock of the Acropolis, on the north side, is the Areopagus, a steep hill close to which was located the court that passed sentences on crimes of violence in

Odeion of Herodes Atticus, reconstruction of the stage

Athens. A small valley, partly occupied by a residential neighborhood, separates the Acropolis from the Pnyx, the Hill of the Nymphs, and the Hill of the Muses.

On the Hill of the Nymphs, upon which an observatory now stands, stood the **Sanctuary of Zeus and the Nymphs.** Nearby, on another hill known as the Hill of the Muses (Mouseion), is the **Funerary Monument of Gaius Antiochos Philopappus,** a descendent of the sovereigns of the Kingdom of Commagene in Asia Minor,

Three Muses from a statue base, ca. 350-330 B.C. (Athens, National Museum)

in what is now southeastern Turkey. The monument was built in Pentelic marble between A.D. 114 and 116 and consisted of a burial chamber and a semicircular façade facing the Acropolis. Decorating the façade's base are reliefs in a clearly Roman style, depicting Philopappus in his capacity as consul. In the upper part of the exedra, three niches contain statues of Philopappus depicted as a philosopher and his ancestors Antiochos IV of Commagene (who ruled between A.D. 38 and 72) and Seleucus Nicator, the last king of

Monument of Philopappos, façade; portrait statues of Philopappos and Antiochos IV; (below) frieze with chariot scene and lictors

Syria; through this desire to represent his ancestors in the statues on his funerary monument Philopappus gained his *co-gnomen*, which means "cherisher of his ancestors." To the north of Philopappus's monument, the hill known as the Pnyx was the location of the citizen's assembly (*ekklesia*) from the age of Kleisthenes, toward the end of the fourth century B.C. The top of the hill was leveled across to make way for a large artificial *cavea*, in front of which stood the tribune (*bema*) from which the

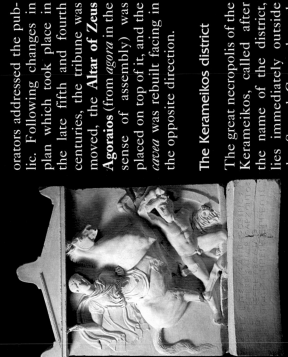

Stele of Dexileos, ca. 394 B.C. (Athens, Kerameikos Museum)

orators addressed the public. Following changes in plan which took place in the late fifth and fourth centuries, the tribune was moved, the **Altar of Zeus Agoraios** (from *agora* in the sense of assembly) was placed on top of it, and the *cavea* was rebuilt facing in the opposite direction.

The Kerameikos district

The great necropolis of the Kerameikos, called after the name of the district, lies immediately outside the Sacred Gate, through which passed the procession to Eleusis on the occa-

Street of the tombs in the Kerameikos

sion of the celebration of the Eleusinian Mysteries, and outside the double gateway (Dipylon) from which the Panathenaic Procession set out.

The most eminent tombs in the Kerameikos are characterized by terraced walls in blocks of stone which contained the burials, at the top of which stood the funerary pieces. These ranged from marble or earthenware vases of colossal dimensions to *stelai* with scenes of farewell or male characters depicted as warriors and female characters engaged in the activities befitting their sex. Beyond the individual and family tombs, there was a special area known as the *demosion sema* (public cemetery) for the burial at the city's expense of those who had distinguished themselves in service to the country.

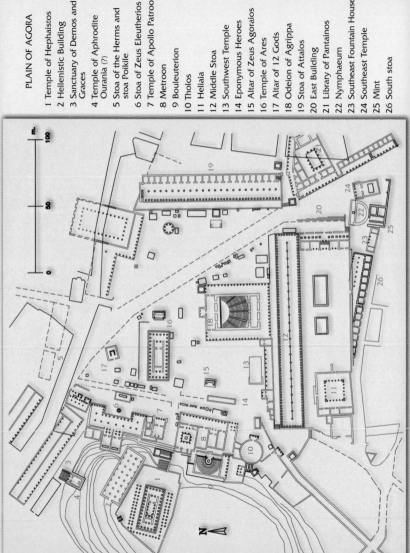

PLAIN OF AGORA

1 Temple of Hephaistos
2 Hellenistic Building
3 Sanctuary of Demos and Graces
4 Temple of Aphrodite Ourania (?)
5 Stoa of the Herms and stoa Poikile
6 Stoa of Zeus Eleutherios
7 Temple of Apollo Patroos
8 Metroon
9 Bouleuterion
10 Tholos
11 Heliaia
12 Middle Stoa
13 Southwest Temple
14 Eponymous Heroes
15 Altar of Zeus Agoraios
16 Temple of Ares
17 Altar of 12 Gods
18 Odeion of Agrippa
19 Stoa of Attalos
20 East Building
21 Library of Pantainos
22 Nymphaeum
23 Southeast Fountain House
24 Southeast Temple
25 Mint
26 South stoa

THE AGORA

To the north of the Acropolis stands the great **Agora** (square) known as the Kerameikos Agora (again after the name of the neighborhood). The entrance to the square was located off the street leading from the Dipylon Necropolis. At the entrance to the agora, on the left for those coming from the Dipylon, is the hill known as the Kolonos Agoraios upon which stands the Hephaisteion (Temple of Hephaistos); the temple is also referred to as the **"Theseion"**, but the attribution to Theseus is mistaken. This is a Doric *peripteral* (i.e., surrounded by columns), with 6 columns across its short sides and 13 down its long ones. The cell is *amphiprostyle* (with columns at both front and back); inside, a two-story colonnade surrounds the space designed to house the statues of the cult of Hephaistos and of Athena Hephaisteia, who, as we know from Pausanias (a writer from the second century A.D. who wrote *Periegesis*, a guidebook with a detailed description of the regions and monuments of Greece), were sculpted by Alkamenes. The perfectly preserved temple, built in the mid-fifth century B.C., still bears the sculpted decorations of its Doric frieze: the metopes on the

The Hephaisteion, above the Agora

east facade depict the Labours of Herakles, and those on the long sides, the Labours of Theseus. A surviving Ionic frieze, proceeding along the inside walls of the *pronaos* and *opisthodomos*, represents Centaurs and Lapiths and scenes from the myth of Theseus. The agora originally occupied a larger area than the current archeological site. The metropolitan line to Piraeus and the Odhos Adrianou cut through the public area, which extended beneath what is now a built-up area, to the north of the modern road. This area is now being excavated by the American School of Archaeology. Here stood the **Stoa Poikile** (painted), so called after the paintings by Polygnotos which it contained, depicting scenes of mythic battles (between Athenians and Amazons, and between Greeks and Trojans), and also historical ones, such as the Battle of Marathon. Toward the end of the fourth century B.C., the Stoa went on to become the seat of Zeno's school of philosophy, which was called the "Stoic" school of philosophy after the name of the place where teachers and students gathered. Another building located in this area is the **Stoa of the Herms**, which is so called because the surrounding area was occupied by a large number of *herms* (ithyphallic half-figures of Hermes, represented with a large erect phallus); these and many other herms scattered throughout the city were mutilated in 415 B.C. on the eve of the departure of the Athenian expedition against Syracuse. The Athenian general Alkibiades was among those accused of this sacrilegious act and was thus forced to go into exile.

The **Stoa Basileios** (royal stoa), a portico with eight Doric columns across the front, was the seat of the magistrate known as the *archon basileus* (king archon) whose function it was to control the laws. Here murder suits were tried and magistrates were sworn in. Inscriptions of the laws of Drako and Solon were also preserved here. The king (*basileus*) carried out mainly religious offices. Not far from the Stoa Basileios is a square precinct with a well in the center; this has been identified, thanks to the finding in the well of inscriptions regarding the cavalry of the Athenian army, as the Leokoreion, the place where Harmodios and Aristogeiton killed Hipparchos, son of Peisistratos. The Tyrannicides were represented in a famous sculpted group by

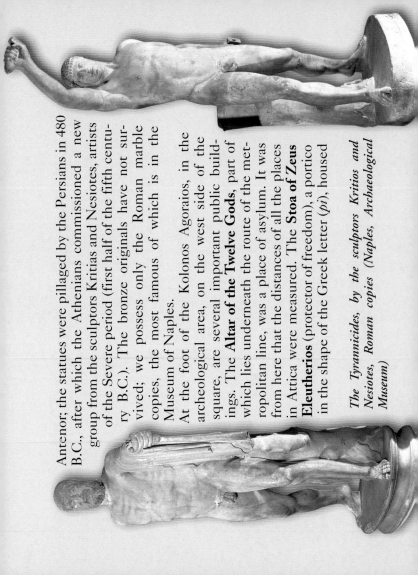

Antenor; the statues were pillaged by the Persians in 480 B.C., after which the Athenians commissioned a new group from the sculptors Kritias and Nesiotes, artists of the Severe period (first half of the fifth century B.C.). The bronze originals have not survived; we possess only the Roman marble copies, the most famous of which is in the Museum of Naples.

At the foot of the Kolonos Agoraios, in the archeological area, on the west side of the square, are several important public buildings. The **Altar of the Twelve Gods**, part of which lies underneath the route of the metropolitan line, was a place of asylum. It was from here that the distances of all the places in Attica were measured. The **Stoa of Zeus Eleutherios** (protector of freedom), a portico in the shape of the Greek letter (*pi*), housed

The Tyrannicides, by the sculptors Kritios and Nesiotes, Roman copies (Naples, Archaeological Museum)

the statues of the Roman emperors who defended the freedom of Greece and a sculpted group depicting Eirene and Ploutos (Peace and Wealth). In the Roman period, a building with two twin areas for the cult of Augustus and Rome was erected behind the stoa. In front of the stoa are the foundations of a temple that has been indentified as the **Temple of Ares**, built by the same architect as the Temple of Poseidon at Cape Sounion, the Temple of Nemesis at Rhamnous, and the Temple of Hephaistos ("Theseion") on the Kolonos Agoraios. It seems that the building was originally located in Acharnai, a *demos* (district) not far from Athens, and that it was dismantled and brought to the Agora during the reign of Augustus. The **Temple of Apollo Patroos**, dedicated to the father of the race of the Ionians, to which the Athe-

nians belonged, was the place where the births of Athenian citizens were registered. The sacred statue of the god, sculpted by Euphranor around the middle of the fourth century B.C., is kept in the Agora Museum. The **Metroon**, the sanctuary of the Mother of the Gods, which also housed the cult of the Kabiroi (associated with the Dioskouroi), stands next to the **Bouleuterion**, a rectangular area with a central *area* that seated those participating in the Assembly of the Five Hundred, the *bouleutai* (councillors elected to represent the tribes). Joined to the Bouleuterion was the **Prytaneion**, the building of the *prytaneis*, those who chaired the Boule, erected a little before the middle of the fifth century B.C. Also known as the "Tholos," it was a circular building where the *prytaneis* lived for the duration of their office. Beneath the

"Tholos" was a lozenge-shaped building (no longer visible) similar to the Regia (royal palace) in the Forum of Rome. This has been identified as the Archaic Prytaneion and also as the residence of the Tyrants (Peisistratos and his family).

In front of the Bouleuterion stands the **Altar of the Eponymous Heroes**, dedicated to the heroes after whom the tribes of Athens were named by Kleisthenes. Here were published the laws and decrees of the city. The building consisted of a rectangular base of marble, 21 meters (69 feet) long, upon which stood the statues of the heroes. Next to it is the **Altar of Zeus Agoraios**, protector of the Agora.

The central area of the square is occupied by a temple of the Augustan period and by the large **Odeion of Agrippa**, a building for concerts, erected at the end of the first century B.C. A spacious square hall contained a *cavea* for an audience of about a thousand, the orchestra, and the stage building. The entrance consisted of a *propylon* through which were two long entrance halls. The building was surrounded by a large colonnade and was connected to what is known as the **Middle Stoa**, which dates to the second century B.C. and is a almost 150 meters (492 feet) long, with a double Doric colonnade; this has recently been identified as a gymnasium.

Further to the south the square was closed by another large stoa, known as the **South Stoa**, built partly in the late Classical period and partly in the Hellenistic age.

The Agora is closed on its east side by the **Stoa of Attalos**, which dates to the mid-second century B.C. This is a portico about 116 meters (380 feet) long, con-

Agora, reconstruction of the south side with Agrippa's Odeion

taining shops built on two stories, with a double portico, Doric and Ionic (inside) on the ground floor and Ionic and Pergamene (inside) on top. In the middle of the facade is the marble base upon which stood a bronze statue depicting the *quadriga* (four-horse chariot) of Attalos II King of Pergamon, who had the monument built at his own expense.

The Stoa of Attalos, which has been rebuilt by the archaeologists of the American School, currently houses the Agora Museum.

To the east of the Stoa of Attalos are the monuments of the Roman Agora, in an area occupied by a square that pre-dates the building of the Stoa of Attalos.

Still further north is the **Library of Hadrian**, built by the Roman emperor in A.D. 132. Entrance is through a Propylon, to the sides of which are two Corinthian colonnades. Inside, a covered portico, decorated with columns of Phrygian marble, surrounded a central courtyard with a large pool in the middle. The library consisted of an enormous hall with niches for books (at the time papyrus rolls) on different levels, connected by ladders and served by walkways. At the back is an area for philosophical discussions and an auditorium for public readings.

The **Roman Agora**, to the south of Hadrian's library, is a porticoed square accessed by a Doric Propylon with four columns on its facade (the Gate of Athena Archegetis, "the founder," upon which is still visible the emperor Hadrian's inscription of dedication).

The north side of the square is occupied by a series of shops. To the east of the square stands an interesting monument known as the **Tower of the Winds**, or the

Horologion of Andronikos. This is an octagonal building that contained the machinery controlling a hydraulic clock. The outer walls form part of a weathervane. On each side is a high relief depicting the wind blowing from that direction (Boreas from the north, Zephyros from the west, Notos from the south, and Apeliotes from the east; Skiron from the northwest, Lips from the southwest, Euros from the southeast, and Kaikias from the northeast). The dating of the building and of the reliefs of the winds are the object of discussion, but the clock was certainly built by the first century B.C., as it is mentioned in Vitruvius's study of architecture.

Tower of the Wind or Horologion of Andronikos, mid 1st century B.C.

THE OLYMPIEION

Along the valley of the Ilissos, to the east of the Roman agora, stands the **Arch of Hadrian,** a single-arched gateway, with a facade consisting of two lateral pilaster strips and two Corinthian columns and surmounted by a small pediment, through which one reaches the area where the colossal **Temple of Zeus Olympios** (Olympieion) must have stood. The construction of this building, the original plan of which was developed in the sixth century B.C. by the family of Peisistratos, was never completed. Only a few traces of the foundations of a monument about 30 meters (98 feet)

Olympieion at the time of the emperor Hadrian, reconstruction

wide and twice as long have been found. Antiochos IV of Syria undertook the construction of a new building, a little before the middle of the second century B.C., which was entrusted to the famous architect Cossutius, but this too was left unfinished.

The surviving temple dates to the reign of Hadrian (A.D. 124–132) and stands in the center of an imposing *temenos* (sacred precinct). Forty-four meters (144 feet) wide and 110 meters (361 feet) long, it is a Corinthian temple, surrounded by a triple colonnade originally consisting of 104 columns, with a long, narrow *naos* (cell), which contained the chryselephantine statue of the god.

Arch of Hadrian, ca. 132 A.D.

The **National Museum of Archaeology** contains an impressive number of masterpieces of Greek art. The opulent collection contains: the golden burial masks and other precious objects from the burial treasures of the royal tombs of the necropolis of Mycenae; the Cycladic idols depicting musicians; the Minoan frescoes of Santorini, the Aegean island destroyed in the second millennium B.C. by an awesome volcanic eruption; the Dipylon-Amphora, a large vase standing over 1.5 meters (5 feet), decorated with geometric motifs and a band depicting funeral scenes, which, according to Greek custom, had served to mark a tomb in the Dipylon Necropolis; the stat-

Amphora from the Dipylon (ca. 750 B.C.) and fragment of vase with funerary scene (ca. 550–540 B.C.)

ures of *kouroi* (full standing figures of young males depicted in heroic nudity) and *korai* (girls wearing *peplos*); funerary monuments or *agalmata* (gifts to the gods); and the bronze statue of Poseidon, found in the sea near Cape Artemision in Euboea.

The **Acropolis Museum** contains sculptures from the decorations of the monuments on the rock and the

The Calf-Bearer and the bronze Poseidon from Cape Artemision, in the background hockey players

votive statues dedicated to the gods of the sanctuaries on the Acropolis; the small museum located in the archaeological area is currently being replaced with a building under construction at the foot of the rock. The works kept in the museum include: the pediments from the Acropolis's Archaic temples, which are in *poros* (local limestone) and painted with lively colours, depicting Herakles fighting the Hydra of Lerna, a lion savaging a bull, and Herakles fighting the sea monster Triton; "Kritios" boy (ca. 490-480 B.C.), the bronze boy from Marathon (ca. 340-300 B.C.), and the Kore 684

the *korai* (representations of girls with richly and finely decorated clothes) dedicated to Athena; the few fragments of the decoration of the Parthenon to have remained in Athens; and the Caryatids from the loggia of the Erechtheion.

The **Agora Museum** contains the findings from the archeological area of the square: the most interesting of these are the *ostraka*, ceramic fragments bearing the scratched names of citizens to be condemned to exile (ostracism) by public vote. Included are the names of important fifth-century Athenian public figures, such as Aristides, Themistokles, and Kimon.

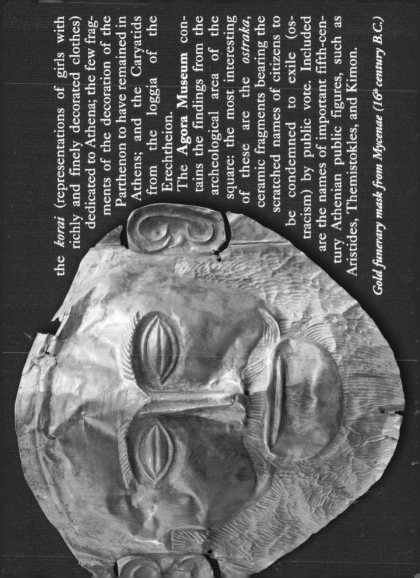

Gold funerary mask from Mycenae (16th century B.C.)

CAPE SOUNION

The Sanctuary of Poseidon at Cape Sounion stands on a high promontory in the southernmost reaches of Attica. In a prominent position on the promontory, the temple was the first and last visible sight of Attica for anyone arriving or leaving by sea. It was used as a place of worship from at least the end of the eighth century B.C.

In the Odyssey, Homer mentions it as the "sacred promontory" where Menelaos's pilot Phrontis was shipwrecked. A well not far from the temple has been found to contain fragments of Archaic statues of *kouroi* and of *korai*, also used to mark tombs, datable to the end of the seventh century B.C. and now kept in the National Museum of Athens.

Temple of Poseidon, detail of the colonnade

At the foot of the hill, by the sea, stood the settlement of Sounion, one of Attica's wealthiest *demoi* (geographical units into which first Attica and later the City of Athens was divided). This was where the regattas took place during the Lesser Panathenaea, annual celebrations in honor of Athena. It enjoyed a position of strategic importance for the control of communications between Athens and the silver mines of Laurion and the shipping routes toward the Islands of the Aegean and Euboea. Some houses of the inhabited area, dating from the fifth century B.C. to the Roman period, survive, as does a section of road, the *agora* (square), and part of the enceinte, which dates back to approximately the end of the fifth century B.C. and is flanked by towers at regular intervals. A small arsenal was big enough to contain two ships.

On the lower part of the hill stands a small *temenos* (sacred precinct), devoted to Athena Sounias, inside which may be seen the foundations of two temples. The larger of these dates to a little after the middle of the fifth century B.C. and is remarkable for having columns only along one of its short sides (10) and one of its long sides (12); a small *pronaos* (antechamber) preceded the *naos* (cell). the main room, which contained the base of the sacred statue, probably Athena. Of the smaller temple, to the north of the Temple of Athena, which may have been a shrine to the hero Phrontis, are preserved the bases of the columns along the front, the marble threshold, and the base of the statue in blue marble from Eleusis.

Access to the **Temenos of Poseidon** was from the north side of the hill. The sanc-

Temple of Poseidon at Cape Sounion, reconstruction

tuary was entered through a Propylon, next to which was a double portico with marble benches; a ramp led up to the temple, which was erected a little after the middle of the fifth century B.C. over the remains of an older temple, which must have been started around 490 B.C. and was destroyed by the Persians in 480 B.C. Beneath the base of the later temple we may see the foundations and stairway of the previous one, in *poros* (local limestone). The temple seen today is a *peripteros* (surrounded by columns on all sides) in marble from the nearby quarries of Agrileza, with 13 fluted Doric columns on the long sides and 6 on the short sides. The columns have only 16 flutes instead of the traditional 20, which gives them a more slender appearance. Inside the colonnade is the cell, which is divided into three parts according to standard practice: *pronaos*, *naos* (where the statue of the god was kept), and *opisthodomos*. The plan, proportions, and style are similar to those of the Temple of Nemesis in Rhamnous, to the Temple of Ares in Athens, and to the Hephaisteion, which suggests that the four temples were the work of the same architect.

The area in front of the *pronaos* must originally have been decorated with scenes of battle against the Centaurs and Giants and scenes of the life of Theseus; some blocks of the frieze are visible in the fortifications to the left of the ramp leading up to the temple.

One of the floral *acroteria* is kept in the National Museum in Athens, but the sculpted decorations on the pediment have been lost.

AEGINA

Aegina is a volcanic island in the Saronic Gulf, lying midway between Attica and the Peloponnese. It was inhabited in pre-historic and Mycenean times, and subsequently colonized by a people from the Peloponnese, possibly Epidauros. Thanks to its geographical position, it conquered a primary role in sea trade; in fact, the Aeginetan system of weights and measures is the most ancient known in Greece. The silver coinage of Aegina bore the image of a tortoise and was thus referred to as "tortoises," or *chelonai*; it was one of the first to be minted in Greece, and is to be found throughout the Mediterranean. A rival of Athens from the early sixth century onwards, Aegina entered the Peloponnesian League and became an

Aegina, aerial view of the excavations

ally first of Sparta, then of Thebes, and then of the Persians, in order to oppose the growing power of Athens. Aegina defeated Athens in a naval battle in 488 B.C., but was forced to admit defeat about 30 years later when Athens, in alliance with Corinth, made the island its colony in 431 B.C., after expelling the last inhabitants.

The main sites on the island are the Temple of Apollo, at Cape Colonna, and the Sanctuary of Aphaia. Of the **Temple of Apollo,** which was built at the end of the sixth century B.C. (530–500) upon the ruins of an older temple, only one column remains in place (hence the name of the locality). This is a Doric temple built in local limestone, with a colonnade consisting of 6 columns across the short sides and 12 down the long ones, and a cell divided into three sec-

tions. The base and part of the decoration of the pediment are still visible. To the southeast of the temple are the remains of an Archaic Propylon, the walls of which are decorated with reliefs and at the center of which is an altar. The building has been identified as the **Aiakeion,** the place of worship of the hero Aiakos (Ajax), son of Zeus and of the nymph Aegina after whom the island was named. Nearby are two small *naiskoi* (shrines) and a circular building that can perhaps be identified as the tomb of the hero Phokos (son of a king of Aegina killed due to the jealousy of his brothers during an athletic contest), which is mentioned by Pausanias. Further to the west is another temple devoted to the dynastic cult of Attalos II King of Pergamon, whose dynasty held sway in Aegina between A.D. 210 and 133.

Temple of Aphaia at Aegina, reconstruction

The **Sanctuary of Aphaia** is a place of worship dedicated to a deity that, judging from the sculptures on the pediment, was probably Athena. However, an inscription of dedication refers to the "*oikos* [house] of Aphaia," and it is probable that the temple was devoted to Athena, but that the local population had assimilated her to the local deity, who may be of Cretan origin. The site had been used as a place of worship since the 25th century B.C., as testified by the finding of small Mycenean idols. The plan of the sanctuary took shape toward the end of the eighth century, when the sacred area, flanked by a building that has been identified as the "house of the priests," was designed to enclose a terrace with a central altar and a cistern. The construction of the *propylon* dates to the seventh century B.C., and perhaps the building of a first temple. In 580 B.C. the terrace was enlarged and a second altar was built, together with a stone Doric temple that may have been *tetrastyle* (with four columns across the front) or distyle *in antis* (with two columns in the middle and the walls of the *pronaos* advancing to the same level). Later, a votive monument, consisting of a column surmounted by a statue of a sphinx, was added.

The monumental phase visible today was constructed following a fire; the "house of the priests" was rebuilt outside the *temenos* and a new distyle *propylon* was erected with octagonal columns, through which one entered the sacred area, where the altar was connected to the temple via a large ramp. The new temple, in stuccoed local limestone, is a Doric peripteral, with 6 columns across the short sides and 11 down the long ones.

The *naos* (cell) is divided into three aisles by double-story colonnades each consisting of five columns, and may be reached both via the *pronaos* and via the *opisthodomos*, which are both distyle *in antis*. The roof, which is covered in marble tiles in the visible parts, was decorated with central *akroteria* in the form of *korai* and side *akroteria* in the form of sphinxes. The pediments were decorated by sculptures.

Discovered in 1811, the sculptures were purchased by King Ludwig I of Bavaria and restored and completed by the famous 18th-century sculptor Thorwaldsen. They are currently kept in the Glyptotek at Munich, where Thorwaldsen's restorations were removed about 30 years ago. The pediments were probably created in two separate phases.

The west pediment, which may be traced to the late Archaic period, depicts duels taking place before Athena during the expedition of Achilles and Agamemnon against Troy.

The east pediment, which also shows scenes of fighting between warriors as Athena watches on, seems to refer to Herakles's expedition against Troy and exhibits the characteristics of the Severe style, datable to the 480 B.C.

Two small buildings on either side of the altar contained other figures, which probably came from the original east pediment, that were sculpted in the round and perhaps depicted the rape by Zeus of the nymph Aegina and scenes of battle against the Amazons.

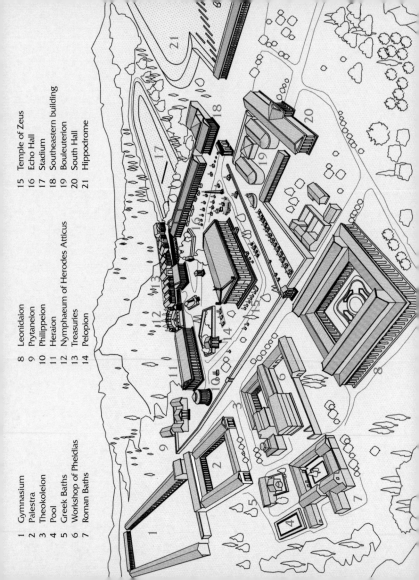

1 Gymnasium
2 Palestra
3 Theokoleion
4 Pool
5 Greek Baths
6 Workshop of Pheidias
7 Roman Baths

8 Leonidaion
9 Prytaneion
10 Philippeion
11 Heraion
12 Nymphaeum of Herodes Atticus
13 Treasuries
14 Pelopion

15 Temple of Zeus
16 Echo Hall
17 Stadium
18 Southeastern building
19 Bouleuterion
20 South Hall
21 Hippodrome

OLYMPIA

The sanctuary of Olympia is one of the most important sanctuaries in the Greek world. The first traces of its plan date back to the eighth century B.C. Legend has it that it was founded by Pelops, the hero after whom the Peloponnese was named, who defeated King Oinomaos in a chariot race, the prize for which was the hand of his daughter Hippodameia. According to another legend, it was Herakles who founded the games and the custom of donning an olive wreath upon victory in the games. According to legend, first Olympic games in ancient times were celebrated in 776 B.C., then on taken as a starting point for the Greek system of dating. As still happens today, the games took place every four years in August (but at the time lasted only five

Amphora depicting long-distance runners, detail

days), with the participation of athletes from all the cities of the Greek world. The first Olympic sport was the running of the *stadion* (measure of distance equivalent to about 192 meters/630 feet), to which other athletic contests were later added, such as the jump and the hurling of the javelin and the discus. The umpires of the games were priest-judges, known as *hellanodikai*, of whom two were initially elected and later ten from 472 B.C. onwards. The importance of the Olympic games was such that wars were suspended while they were taking place. The sanctuary enjoyed wealth and prestige until

Aerial view of Olympia today

t was sacked by Sulla during the Roman conquest in 86 B.C. Its end was marked by the fourth-century edicts of the Roman Emperor Theodosius, who forbade the execution of pagan practices and events.

The Altis

The Sacred Grove was known as the Altis, and it was frequented from the early eighth century B.C, as we know from the votive offerings found there (small statues, vases, bronze objects). The first monumental phase of the sanctuary, represented by the Temple of Hera, took place

Bronze plate with Centauromachy (Olympia Museum)

between the middle and the end of the seventh century; in the next century the first version of the stadium was completed, along with the first *bouleuterion* (building for meetings) and the first *thesauroi* (treasuries erected by the communities for their offerings to the sanctuary), dedicated by the Greek colonies of South Italy and Sicily (Sybaris, Metapontum, Gela). The dedication of the great votive offerings (votive statues which often referred to the world of athleticism in the case of Olympia) also dates back to the end of the sixth century. The building activity in the Sanctuary of Olympia, founded by the city of Elis, in whose territory it was situated, was very intense in the period between the Persian Wars and the Peloponnesian War, when the sanctuary was enriched with masterpieces of Greek sculpture that have now almost all been

Zeus and Ganymede, terra-cotta group, ca. 475-470 B.C. (Olympia, Museum)

lost. Among the most famous sculptures were the golden shield dedicated to the Spartans on the Temple of Zeus, and the chryselephantine (gold and ivory) cult statue of the god, sculpted by Pheidias. A violent earthquake in 374 B.C. and the clashes between the Eleans and the Arcadians in 364 B.C. caused serious devastation in the sanctuary. When Elis recovered control shortly afterwards, there was a resumption of building activity, which included the erection of the *zanes* (images of Zeus, undertaken at the expense of athletes fined for breaking the rules of

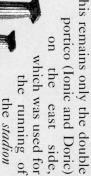

The Palaestra, detail of the colonnade

the contests). Access to the sanctuary, which lies inside a rectangular precinct, is currently at the northwest corner, where there are two monuments from the Hellenistic age: the gymnasium and the palaestra. The **Gymnasium** was built toward the end of the third century B.C. and was where training took place. Of this remains only the double portico (Ionic and Doric) on the east side, which was used for the running of the *stadion* indoors, and the Doric portico on the north side of the palaestra, which was used for wrestling and boxing. The **Palaestra**, a square building built at the beginning of the third century B.C., is organized around a big *peristyle* (courtyard surrounded by a colonnaded portico), onto which open a series of rooms that had different functions; there are indoor exercise, a changing room, and a place where the solemn meetings of the athletes took place (*ephebeion*), along with the storerooms for the oil and sand used by the athletes, and the bathing area. To the south of the palaestra stands a group of buildings: a series of rooms opening

onto a paved courtyard that was perhaps the **Theokoleion**, the priests' house; another *palaestra*, built in classical times, that may have later become the temporary residence of the sanctuary attendants; and the so-called **Heroon**, a building constructed in the fifth century B.C., consisting of a portico through which one passes into a rectangular room and another area in which several inscriptions have been found with dedications to a hero whose identity is unknown. In front of the *heroon* is a bathing establishment (the Greek Baths), which was replaced in Roman times by another one called the Kladeos Baths after the nearby south-flowing river. The Greek Baths were

Head of a boxer; bronze (Athens, National Museum)

equipped with a long hall for baths and ablutions to which was later added a room with an apse (i.e., one of its short sides was semi-circular) with a *hypocaust* (a heating system consisting of a hollow space under the floor) for hot baths; there was a pool (*kolymbethra*) for swimming and cold plunges. The Kladeos Baths were built toward A.D. 100, and two buildings were later added (between the end of the second century and first two decades of the third century) to house important guests. The baths were paved throughout in mosaic, and comprised a sequence of rooms: the *atrium*; a storage room; and a *frigidarium*, off which were small rooms for individual baths; the *apodyterium* (changing room); the *laconicum* (circular sweat bath); the *tepidarium* (place for warm bathing); and the *calidarium* (place for hot bathing).

To the east of the baths stands a building that was transformed into a Byzantine church in the fifth century A.D.; this was the **Workshop of Pheidias**, a rectangular structure decorated with architectural

The Byzantine church built on the ruins of the workshop of Pheidias (detail)

decorations in terracotta, flanked by outhouses (perhaps storerooms) where the pieces discarded in the sculpting of the famous 12-meter (39-foot) gold and ivory statue of Zeus have been found. The statue, for which a ton of gold was probably used, was created using a technique that involved the carving of a wooden frame, often from precious wood, onto which were mounted the robes in gold and the visible parts of the body in ivory (from an elephant or hippopotamus).

To the south of Pheidias's workshop is a big rectangular building, the **Leonidaion,** which takes its name from its benefactor, Leonidas of Naxos. It was built around the middle of the fourth century B.C. and served as a hotel. Surrounded by Ionic porticoes with architectural decorations in terracotta, it is organized around a central courtyard with a Doric colonnade, off which there are several rooms, including bathing areas and kitchens with sophisticated plumbing. Next to the Leonidaion stands a **small bathing establishment** which may be dated to the first century A.D., in all probability reserved for the guests in residence; nearby to the south and east are another two Roman bathing establishments.

This area must have been the original entrance to the sanctuary, on the site of the agora mentioned by Pausanias. In front of the northeast corner of the Leonidaion stands an ornamental gateway, the starting point for the solemn procession which inaugurated the games.

To the east of the bathing establishments are two public buildings, which may have been archives, and the **Bouleuterion** (building where the meetings of the *boule*, or council, took place), which was

Olympia, detail of the Bouleuterion

Olympia, detail of the Bouleuterion built in various phases between the sixth and the fourth century B.C. The *bouleuterion* consists of an Ionic portico through which one enters a square hall, next to which are two rectangular halls with apses, which may have been used for worship. At the end of these halls were two rooms that are thought to have been

thalamoi; the safest room in the house, the *thalamos* is where the family kept its treasure. There may have been two halls because it was under the joint control of Elis and Pisa, another city in the western Peloponnese. To the south of the *bouleuterion* stands a large double portico, the "South Hall," with a Doric colonnade on the outside and a Corinthian one on the inside, from which one could view the inaugural procession of the games.

Toward the east end of the sanctuary stands an imposing monumental complex known as the **Echo Hall**, or *stoa heptaphonos* (of the seven voices), due to the echo that is to be heard inside; according to the Roman historian and writer Pliny, the sounds were repeated seven times. It is also known as the Stoa Poikile (painted stoa) after the paintings it contained, according to Pausanias. The construction of the portico was started in the mid-fourth century and it is almost 100 meters (328 feet) long. Like the South Hall. Echo Hall originally had two colonnades: one Doric and one Corinthian (even though, according to some, there were only columns on the facade, and pilasters inside).

In front of the portico stand several votive bases and the monument dedicated to the Egyptian Kings Ptolomy II and Arsinoe by the Commander of the Fleet Kallikrates, in the first half of the third century B.C.

Echo Hall

The monument consists of a base with columns surmounted by statues.

Behind the Echo Hall is a **bathing establishment** which stands on the remains of a large Roman house, in turn built on the remains of a building dating back to the fifth century B.C. that may be the **Sanctuary of Hestia**, where the sacred fire was guarded.

The central hall of the baths, which is octagonal in shape, was decorated in polychrome marble and a mosaic depicting the triumph of Zeus and Amphitrite, with a following of marine animals.

To the south of the baths was a sanctuary

dedicated to Artemis, which may be dated to the fifth century B.C.

A door leads into a vaulted tunnel and thence into the **Stadium**, the track of which measured exactly one *stadion* (600 feet, or about 192 meters). It consisted of a large earthwork, with room for about 40,000 spectators, and stands for the judges. In the west of the current one (constructed in the last 30 years of the fourth century B.C.), the track started from the Altar of Zeus; the votive bronzes, that originally decorated the trophies placed along the embankments which served as stands, date back to the building of the fifth century B.C.

The Entrance to the Stadium

View of the Stadium

THE NYMPHAEUM OF HERODES ATTICUS

To the west of the stadium are the **Treasuries**, or *thesauroi*, a terrace containing a row of shrines designed to hold the votive offerings dedicated to Olympia by the cities of Greece, and those of its colonies in particular. There remain about fifteen of these buildings, described by Pausanias, including those of the Sicilian cities Gela, Selinous, Megara Hyblaia, and Syracuse; those of Metapontum and Sybaris (South Italy); and those of Epidamnos (Epirus), Cyrene (Libya), and Byzantium (now Istanbul). The most ancient treasury is that of Sikyon, built in the sixth century B.C. Worthy of note are the architectural terracotta decorations of the Thesauros of Gela and the sculptures decorating that of Megara Hyblaia, which depict a *gigantomachia* (Battle against the Giants).

In the same area stood the **Nymphaeum of Herodes Atticus,** built in the second century A.D. This is an ornamental fountain, which collected the waters of a large aqueduct originating in the nearby mountains, consisting of a rectangular basin and a larger semicircular one, the curved wall of which contained evenly spaced columns and niches for statues of members of the Roman Imperial Antonine dynasty and of the family of Herodes Atticus. The most impressive of these statues is that of the wife of Herodes Atticus, Annia Regilla.

As priestess of Demeter, she donated a statue of a bull to the sanctuary; it was originally located in the nymphaeum, and is now kept in the Olympia Museum. The nymphaeum stands on the remains of two shrines dedicated to Aphrodite Ourania and a deity termed Sosipolis (savior of the city).

Nymphaeum of Herodes Atticus, reconstruction

THE HERAION

At the foot of the terrace is the *Metroon*, a peripteral Doric temple, with 6 columns across the short sides and 11 down its long sides, dating back to the fourth century B.C. and dedicated to Rheia, mother of the gods.

Not far from the Metroon, near the place where the Altar of Hera still stands, originally stood the Altar of Zeus. We know from Pausanias that it was built from the ashes of sacrifices and that every year it was replastered with ash from the Prytaneion mixed with water from the river Alphaios, one of the two rivers sacred to Zeus which flows past the sanctuary (the other is the Kladeos).

The **Heraion**, or Temple of Hera, is the oldest sacred building in the sanctuary. It was built in the mid-seventh century B.C. An initial restoration dates back to

around 600 B.C. It is a Doric peripteral temple, with 6 columns across the back and front and 16 down the long sides, which are considerably longer than usual. The *pronaos* and *opisthodomos* are distyle *in antis* (i.e., they had two columns on the facade in between the ends of the walls); the base of the cell was in stone and the elevated parts in rough brickwork. Each aisle was divided into four areas by columns at the sides on two stories. The columns were originally of wood, one of which, in oak, still survived, once more according to Pausanias, at the time of his writing (in the second century A.D.).

In the *opisthodomos*, the back room of the temple, were kept the *agalmata* (precious objects received by the sanctuary as votive offerings): a table in gold and ivory, decorated with mythological scenes, which was used for the awarding of prizes to the athletes; a wooden box,

Facade of the Heraion, reconstruction

with gold and ivory inlay, known as the Chest of Kypselos, donated by Kypselos Tyrant of Corinth who reigned over the isthmus city in the late seventh century B.C.; and such famous statues as Hermes with Dionysos as a boy sculpted by Praxiteles (a famous sculptor of the late Classical period, active around the mid-fourth century, between 370 and 330 B.C.).

THE PHILIPPEION

The Philippeion, erected by Philip II of Macedon after the Battle of Chaironeia (338 B.C.) during which the Macedonian king defeated the Athenians and their allies, stands close to the Heraion. The circular building stood on a base of three steps and had an external colonnade consisting of 18 Ionian columns surrounding the circular cell, the roof of which bore marble tiles, ante-fixes with palmettes, and drip mouldings in the form of lions' heads. The cell's inner

Hermes with the infant Dionysos by Praxiteles, ca. 350–330 B.C. (Olympia, Museum)

Proposed reconstruction of the Philippeion

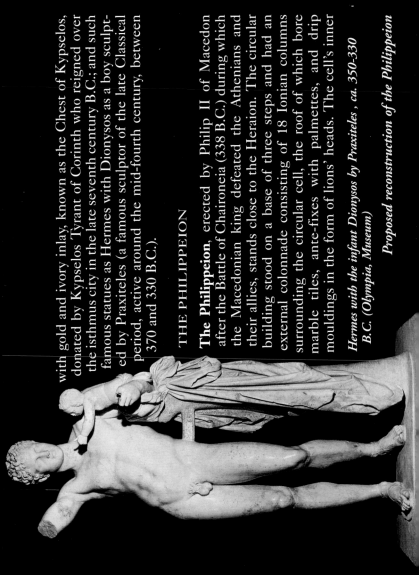

facade was decorated with nine half-columns with Corinthian capitals. The cell itself contained a group of five statues sculpted by the sculptor Leochares, one of the specialists in chryselephantine statues active around the middle of the fourth century B.C. The statues depict members of the Macedo-nian royal family: Philip II, his parents, Amyntas and Eurydike, his wife Olympias, and his son Alexander the Great, who was responsible for the completion of the building after his father's death in 336 B.C.

The **Prytaneion** (the building of the *prytaneis*, administrators of the sanctuary), a square building that was begun toward the end of the sixth century B.C., served as an official reception area. Among other things, it hosted the winners of the games at the sanctuary's expense.

A sacred precinct, the **Pelopion**, almost at the center of the sanctuary, was dedicated to the eponymous hero-king of the Peloponnese. Sacrifices at the start to the games were conducted here; the victim of choice was a black ram, the most high-ly rated victim for heroic sacrifices.

The Pelopion, which already existed in the sixth century B.C., consisted of a poly-gonal *peribolos* (perimeter), entered through a *propylon* with four Doric columns. In the center of the sacred precinct, in the oldest strata, the remains of a tomb have been found; it was com-mon, in the case of *heroa* (monuments to heroes), for the *cenotaph* (memorial tomb) to be located within a sacred precinct.

THE TEMPLE OF ZEUS

In the central area of the sanctuary is the **Temple of Zeus**, which was built by the architect Libon, a native of Elis, with the

Temple of Zeus, inside view with the god's statue, work of Pheidias

city's war booty in the mid-fifth century B.C. (470–457 B.C.). It is a Doric peripteral temple, with 6 columns across the short sides and 13 down the long ones, in local limestone, covered in painted stucco. Parian marble was used for certain parts of the entablature and roof, and for the sculptures decorating the pediment and the metopes on the frieze. The cell had a double colonnade, on two orders or levels, and was divided into two parts by marble balusters painted by Panainos, the famous Athenian painter who may have been the nephew of Pheidias. In front of the black stone base of the sacred statue was a basin with white marble sides which contained the oil necessary for the upkeep of the ivory parts of the statue. As in the Temple of Hera, here too were kept various votive gifts, most of which have been lost, but which survive in Pausanias's description, together with details of the temples decoration, such as the golden *acroteria* (sculptures which decorated the upper parts of the pediment), one in the shape of a *lebes* (cauldron) and another representing Nike (underneath this was the golden shield which the Spartans offered to the god after the Battle of Tanagra). The chryselephantine statue of Zeus, one of

Coin with image of Zeus of Olympia
(Florence, Archaeological Museum)

the seven wonders of the world, depicted the god with Nike in his right hand and a sceptre in his left, seated on an ebony throne decorated with mythological figures and scenes in relief, in the round and encrusted. According to Pausanias, the votive gifts included a four-horse chariot (*quadriga*) donated by the daughter of the Archidamos King of Sparta, a throne offered to the god by Arimnestos King of Etruria and statues of Augustus and Trajan. The temple's metopes and pediments, which are kept in the Museum of Olympia, are regarded as some of the greatest masterpieces of what is known as the Severe

Temple of Zeus, metope with Herakles and Atlas, the god Apollo and details of the sculptures of the west pediment

style (from 500 to about 450 B.C.). They were executed by a sculptor known as the "master of Olympia" between 470 and 460 B.C. The east pediment depicts the preparations for the chariot race between Oinomaos and Pelops (in which the hero defeated the king, thus winning the hand of his daughter Hippodameia) as Zeus, father of the gods, watches on. The west pediment depicts the marriage of the Lapith Peirithoos (who belonged to a primitive tribe that inhabited the mountains of Thessaly), friend of the hero Theseus, to another Hippo-

Temple of Zeus, west pediment:
Deidameia and the centaur Eurytion;
in the background Hercules and the
Cretan bull

dameia (daughter of Butes, one of the Argonauts, Jason's companions), and the battle between the Lapiths and the Centaurs that ensued when the latter got drunk and attempted to abduct the Lapith women, as Apollo watches on. The metopes on the frieze depict the Labours of Herakles: the capture of the boar of Mount Erymanthos, the capture of the horses of Diomedes King of Thrace, the capture of the oxen of Geryon King of Tartessos, the delivery of the apples of the Hesperides to Eurystheos, the capture of Kerberos, the cleaning of the stables of Augeas, the capture of the Nemean lion, the killing of the Hydra of Lerna, the capture of the Cretan bull, the shooting of the birds of Stymphalos, the capture of the hind of Ceryneia, and the delivery of the golden girdle of Hippolyta Queen of the Amazons. A large number of bases for votive statues, some of which are masterpieces of classical art, are to be found in the *peristasis* of the temple and in the surrounding area. Two great votive monuments of the fifth century B.C. were donated by Phormis, general of the tyrants of Syracuse Gelon and Hieron, and by Mikythos, friend of Anaxilas Tyrant of Rhegion (Rhegium) (twelve of the statues of this latter votive monument were still visible in the day of Pausanias). Still visible today is the base of a statue depicting a bull dedicated to Zeus by the inhabitants of Eretria for having escaped destruction by the Persians. Another surviving piece is the semicircular base of the gift of the Achaeans, dated to 470 B.C., which depicts the casting of lots for the selection of the Achaean champion to fight Hector. Nearby is the base of a triangular pilaster depicting Nike in flight; this 420 B.C. work by the sculptor Paionios of Mendes commemorates the role of the inhabitants of Naupaktos (a city in Messenia) in the Battle of Sphakteria, during which the Athenians defeated the Spartans. Another interesting monument is a base upon which, as the inscription reads, stood a colossal statue of Zeus, which was 10 cubits high (4.5 meters/15 feet), dedicated by the cities of Greece that had taken part in the Battle of Plataea against the Persians. This statue was similar to two other *colossi*. The first, measuring 3.5 meters (11 feet) high, was offered by the Spartans to commemorate victory in one of the wars against the Messenians; the inscribed base still remains (the inscription is mentioned by Pausanias). The second is over 8 meters

(26 feet) high, and commemorates the victory of the Eleans over the Arcadians in 362 B.C.

Between the Temple of Zeus and the Bouleuterion also stands the monumental offering of Praxiteles, a citizen of Mantinea who lived in Sicily (in Syracuse and Kamarina) at the beginning of the fifth century B.C. This consists of a marble base that once supported bronzes executed by Aeginetan artists. Nearby is the Monument of Apollonia, a colony of the Corinthians and of the Corcyreans; this was a semicircular marble base with sculptures executed a little after the mid-fifth century B.C. by Lykios, son of Miron, depicting a scene from Trojan cycle: the duel between Achilles and Memnon, as Zeus looks on with the mothers of the heroes, Thetis and Eos.

GLOSSARY

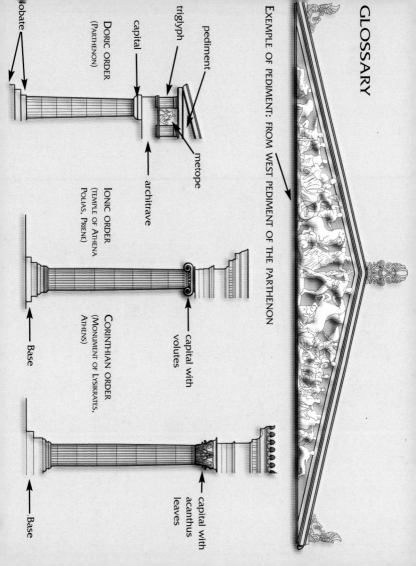

EXAMPLE OF PEDIMENT: FROM WEST PEDIMENT OF THE PARTHENON

pediment

triglyph

capital

DORIC ORDER
(PARTHENON)

metope

architrave

IONIC ORDER
(TEMPLE OF ATHENA
POLIAS, PRIENE)

capital with
volutes

CORINTHIAN ORDER
(MONUMENT OF LYSIKRATES,
ATHENS)

Base

capital with
acanthus
leaves

Base

obate

Text by EMANUELE GRECO, Director of the Italian Archaeological School of Athens

Drawing and reconstructions: Vision S.r.l.

Graphic project and layout: Federico Schneider

Cover: Michael Freeland

Photograph by Scala Group S.p.A, Alinari Picture Library, Laura Ronchi S.r.l, Pubbli
Aer Foto, Tips S.r.l., D.A.I. Athens, Toubis SA, Vision S.r.l

Copyright © 2004 VISION s.r.l.

VISION S.r.l. - Via Livorno, 20 - 00162 Roma - Tel/Fax (39) 0644292688
E-mail: info@visionpubl.com

WILEY PUBLISHING, INC, 111 River Street, Hoboken, NJ 07030

ISBN 0-7645-6823-X

Printed in Italy by Tipolitografica CS - Padova

VISION
S.R.L.
ROMA

PAST & PRESENT®